BUSINESS IN ACTION

COCA-COLA

WILLIAM GOULD

CHERRYTREE BOOKS

ACKNOWLEDGEMENT

Our thanks to The Coca-Cola Company for providing us with copies of their annual reports and historical publications from which we drew information to develop a profile of the Company. Editorial comments made and conclusions reached by the author about general business practices of international companies do not necessarily reflect the policies and practices of The Coca-Cola Company.

CONTENTS

▲ **Businesses need people (human resources), things (physical resources) and money (capital).**

The adventure of business

Business often sounds difficult but its basic principles are simple, and it can be very exciting. The people involved in the creation and running of the businesses we examine in BUSINESS IN ACTION faced challenges and took risks that make some adventure stories seem dull.

What is a business?

If you sell your old football to your friend for money you are making a business deal. Anyone who produces goods or services in return for money, or works for an organization that does so, is involved in business.

Businesses try to make profits. They try to sell things for more than the amount the things cost them to make. They usually invest part of the profit they make to produce and sell more of their products. If they have no money to invest, they may borrow it.

The language of business

Many of the technical terms that make the language of business sound complicated are explained on pages 46/47.

Business matters

Yellow panels throughout the book explain general business concepts. Blue panels tell you more about Coca-Cola.

The Coca-Cola legend

Coca-Cola is more than a drink. It is a major international company. Its advertising slogans and jingles are legendary. It is known and drunk all over the world. Yet, at first, its inventor thought it might not catch on.

▼ **A business uses money to buy human and physical resources, and create a product or service which it sells for a profit.**

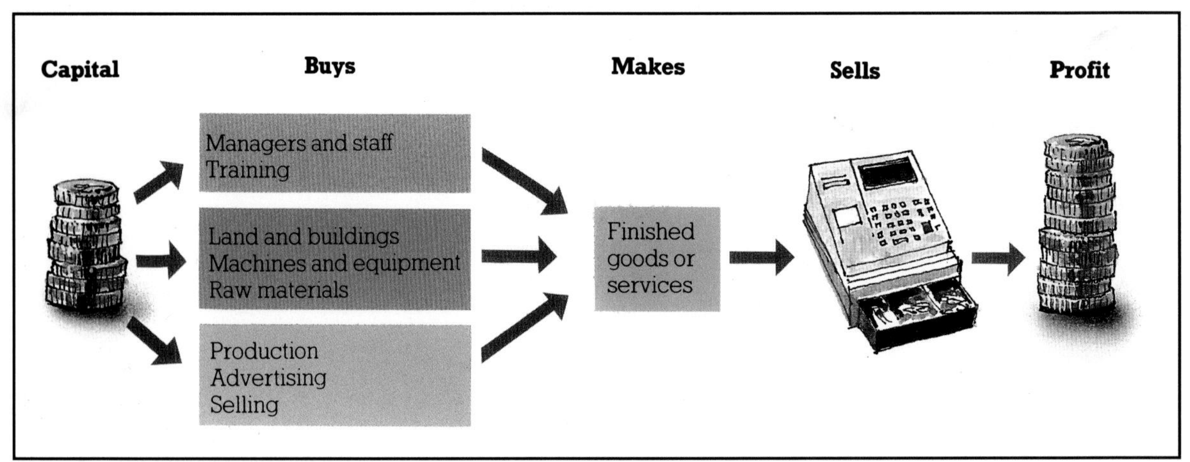

◀ America's most popular president with America's most popular drink. This is the kind of publicity every company wants.

▶ The Coca-Cola Company sells a wide range of products all round the world. This slim lady with a can of diet Coke is from Tahiti.

▼ These are all products of The Coca-Cola Company. All have strong brand images, especially Coca-Cola which has the most recognized trademark in the world.

▼ A streamlined bottling plant. Coca-Cola is bottled or canned in many countries.

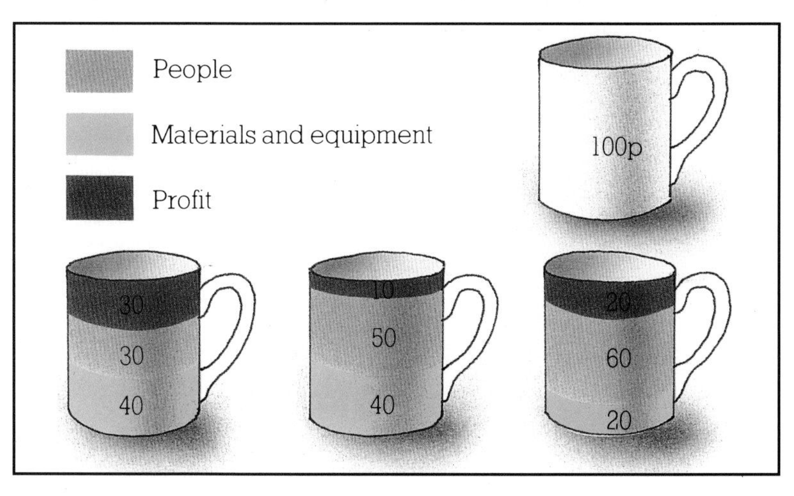

◀ The purpose of a business is to make a profit. Profit is the amount of money earned from sales that remains after all the costs are paid - the higher the costs, the lower the profits. This mug sells for one pound. If it costs 80 pence to make and sell, the profit is 20 pence.

Coca-Cola

What is the mystery of the sweet, brown liquid we know as Coca-Cola? Every second of the day, somewhere in the world there are people drinking Coca-Cola.

The soft-drinks industry includes amongst others lemonade, fizzy orange, mineral water and fruit juices. Coca-Cola, or Coke for short, is the industry's most successful product.

▲ Excellent advertising and choice of products has enabled The Coca-Cola Company to lead the market in soft drinks.

The taste of success

Why is Coca-Cola so successful? There are many reasons: it is dependable. It always tastes exactly as you expect it to. It is easy to afford and easy to find – from Torquay to Timbuktu. Dressed in red and white, with its ribbon curve, a can of Coke is unmistakable. And its advertising jingles ring in your ears.

Thanks to clever selling and advertising over decades, the image of Coke has become part of our lives. But Coke is not the only product that The Coca-Cola Company sells. It produces a variety of soft drinks that together outsell the products of every other soft-drinks company.

The Coca-Cola system

The Coca-Cola Company has its headquarters in Atlanta, Georgia in the United States, but not all the drinks that are

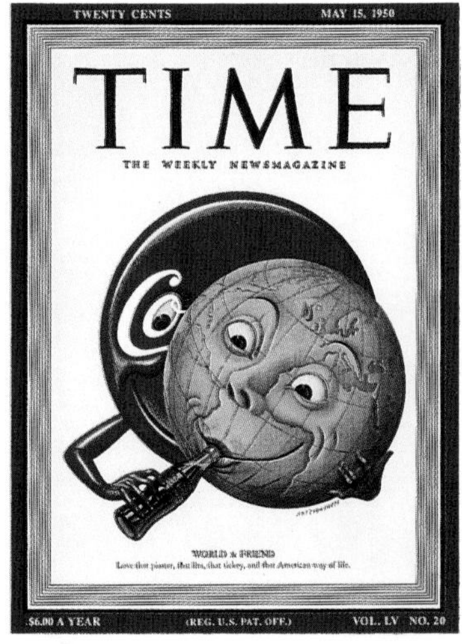

▲ The cover of the May 1950 issue of *Time* magazine shows Coca-Cola as the world's friend.

◀ Whatever the language, a bottle of Coke is instantly recognizable.

sold throughout the world are made there. A network of companies makes and bottles Coca-Cola and other products of The Coca-Cola Company for their local area. They work under licence – and under strict supervision.

The three Ps

For years Coco-Cola's stated aim was to make its products available, affordable and acceptable – the three As. It has now set itself even more ambitious goals – the three Ps. Instead of mere availability, it wants *pervasive penetration* of the market place. Instead of affordability, it intends to give consumers the best *price relative to value*. Instead of mere acceptability, it aims to be the *preferred* beverage everywhere.

FACTS ABOUT COCA-COLA

* It has a market value of almost $93 billion – more than 61,000 million pounds.
* It is the second largest public company in the United States.
* Its headquarters are in Atlanta, Georgia, USA.
* It operates in almost 200 countries.
* It directly employs more than 32,000 people. Many thousands more are employed by franchised bottlers.
* It makes diet Coke, Fanta, Sprite, Lilt and many other products.
* It makes Minute Maid and Five Alive juices in many flavours.
* It once traded in tea, coffee and wine.
* It ships nearly 13 billion cases (24 bottles or cans) every year.
* It has 8 million wholesale customers.
* Its biggest customer is McDonald's, the hamburger chain.
* Its 1995 sales were worth $18 billion – 12 million pounds.
* For a time it owned Columbia Pictures.

◀ **Expensive hand-painted stand-up displays at the 'point of sale' enticed consumers to try a delicious and refreshing glass of Coke.**

The birth of Coca-Cola

The image of Coke is youthful and modern. But Coke is not new. It is more than a century old. It was invented in 1886 by a pharmacist called John Styth Pemberton.

Pemberton had a drugstore in Atlanta, where he sold liver pills, hair restorer, cough mixtures and other medicines. He made these preparations to his own recipes, but people could buy similar products at any drugstore. They loved his Indian Queen hairdye, but there was nothing special about it. Pemberton wanted to make a product that people could buy only from him. He wanted them to have a reason to choose his shop rather than any other.

Needing a tonic

Tonic is a drink that is supposed to do you good. In the old days, many chemists made and sold their own tonic wine. In 1885 Pemberton came up with French Wine Cola. It must have tasted rather like Coke. At first Pemberton put a little alcohol in it, but later he left it out. He is said to have mixed his brew in the backyard in a three-legged brass pot like a witches' cauldron.

Pemberton sold the new drink as a quick cure for headaches. But headaches or no headaches, his staff were soon watering down the syrup and drinking it to slake their thirst on hot days. Maybe he really had invented a new soft drink product.

JOHN STYTH PEMBERTON, 1833-1888

John Styth Pemberton was born in Knoxville, Georgia, USA. As a boy he was interested in science and later studied chemistry at Macon, Georgia. He opened his first shop in Columbus, Georgia, in 1856. But the American Civil War (1861-1865) wrecked his business. After the war, in which he fought on the losing side, Pemberton moved to Atlanta and worked hard to rebuild his business. He set up the Pemberton Chemical Company to research new formulas and manufacture all kinds of medicines and tonics. He always kept his formulas secret. The formula for his Coca-Cola remains a secret to this day. Sadly, Pemberton never knew how successful that particular formula was. Shortly before he died, he sold his secret – because he couldn't sell his product.

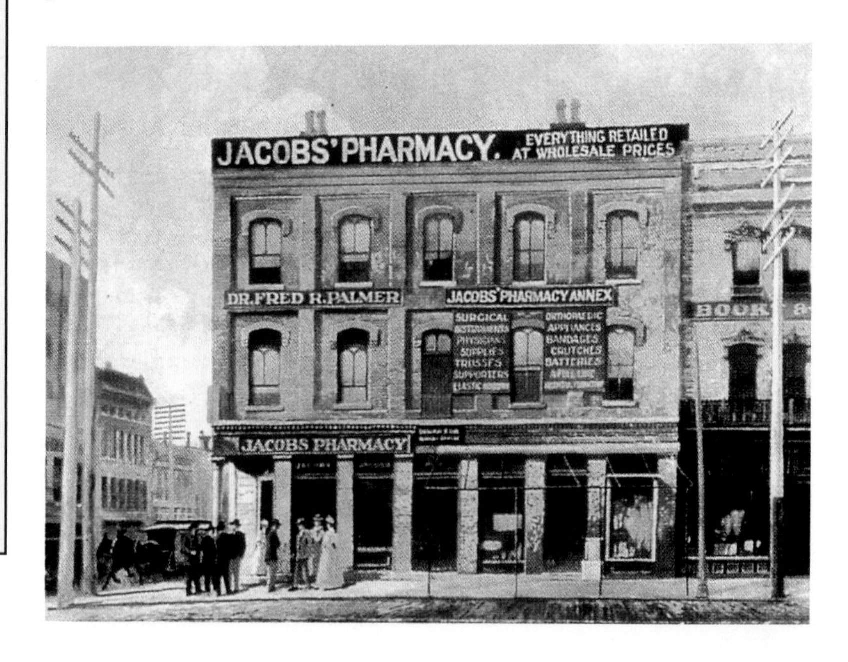

▶ **Pemberton tried out his new tonic in this Atlanta drugstore.**

BUSINESS MATTERS: THE RIGHT PRICE

Some companies are profitable because they sell extremely expensive products to a few people who can afford them. Others are successful because they sell to ordinary people – the mass market – at a price everyone can afford. No matter how refreshing Coca-Cola was, it would not have been a success if Pemberton and his successors had pitched the price too high to attract large numbers of people.

▼ **The first advertisements for Coca-Cola were made of oilcloth or painted on walls. In the first year, sales were $50, advertising costs were $73.96.**

On Saturday 8 May 1886 Pemberton took a jug of syrup down the street to another drugstore, Jacobs' Pharmacy – to do a test.

Adding a sparkle

Jacobs' pharmacy had a soda fountain. This machine adds carbon dioxide to water to make fizzy soda, and then mixes it with syrup to make a refreshing drink. Stalls selling ice cream and fizzy drinks made by soda fountains became known simply as soda fountains.

The staff and customers of Jacobs' pharmacy tried Pemberton's headache cure mixed with soda and loved its taste. It was excellent, but it did not have a name.

One of Pemberton's partners, his book-keeper Frank Robinson, suggested Coca-Cola Syrup and Extract – which became Coca-Cola for short. He thought the two Cs would go well in advertising. He wrote down the name in the simple flowing handwriting that he used in his account books. His script became the product's trademark.

Coca-Cola went on sale immediately at five cents a glass.

BUSINESS MATTERS: A GOOD IDEA

Business people are always looking for good ideas, for gaps in the market – products that people would want if they were available. There was a big demand for thirst-quenching drinks in the hot southern states of America, and no end of people trying to meet the demand. It was the genuinely refreshing taste of Pemberton's invention – coupled with good selling techniques – that made Coca-Cola a success.

ASA GRIGGS CANDLER, 1851-1929

Born on a farm near Villa Rica, Georgia, Asa Candler came to Atlanta after the Civil War. He studied medicine and, like John Pemberton, became a pharmacist. He built up a successful business selling perfumes, toiletries, soap and toothpaste. Then he built The Coca-Cola Company into a giant corporation, which he sold in 1919 for $25 million.

Candler did not keep all his vast wealth. He gave a great deal to charitable causes. He supported Emory University, Atlanta, and donated $2 million to found a teaching hospital next door.

Coca-Cola for sale

John Pemberton knew he had invented a good product but he was not good at selling it. He made the Coca-Cola syrup in his shop and distributed it to local soda fountains. In the first year sales reached at most 13 glasses a day.

Pemberton advertised in the local newspaper and displayed hand-painted oilcloth signs but sales remained sluggish. To raise money, Pemberton gradually sold off parts of his business to his partners, the men who had invested money in his chemical business and helped him over the years.

The Coca-Cola Company

Shortly before his death in 1888, Pemberton sold his remaining share in Coca-Cola, together with the secret formula. The buyer was a go-ahead businessman named Asa G. Candler. The price was $1,200. Candler soon bought out the other partners. By 1891 he owned the whole Pemberton company. He had paid $2,300 in total.

On 29 January 1892, in partnership with his brother John, Frank Robinson and two other men, Candler formed The Coca-Cola Company. The new company with all its assets (equipment and property) and all the business it had from local soda fountains was valued at $100,000 – a vast sum in those days. But Candler was not satisfied. He wanted growth.

Coca-Cola takes off

Candler had a gift for selling and advertising – and for promotion. He distributed coupons that offered people one

BUSINESS MATTERS: CAPITAL & INVESTMENT

To start up a business you need money – financial capital. If you are not wealthy you have to earn the money or borrow it and offer the lender something in return – the money that was loaned to you and some more. You have to convince the lenders that you will not lose their money but use it wisely. Many banks and rich people like to invest in business projects. They contribute money (or some other sort of capital, such as buildings or machinery). Usually they receive a share of the company in exchange for their money. Both Pemberton and Candler had to raise money from investors. To raise the $2,300 he needed to buy Pemberton's company, Candler had to sell other business interests.

▶ **Giving the product away! Vouchers like these, offering a free glass of Coke, were handed out to passers-by. One hundred years later, The Coca-Cola Company still promotes its products by giving away free samples.**

free glass of Coke. He rightly guessed that, once they tasted it, they would be back for more and willing to pay.

By 1894 Candler was selling Coke way beyond Georgia. He opened a syrup-making plant in Dallas, Texas, and then offices and factories in Los Angeles, Chicago and Philadelphia. Coke was soon on sale in every one of the United States. By 1897 it was available in Canada and Hawaii, and shortly afterwards in Mexico. In less than ten years Candler had increased the sales by 400 per cent.

BUSINESS MATTERS: KEEPING ACCOUNT

You always need more money than you imagine when you start a business. Many businesses fail because they have too little capital and do not keep a careful watch on where the money is going. Keeping proper accounts is important. You have to pay for your materials, you have to give credit to customers (time for them to pay), you have to pay for your overheads (premises and so on), you have to pay for development and production costs, you have to pay for advertising, selling and distribution, you have to pay your staff, you have to pay interest to the bank and there are many other calls on the company purse. If you manage to make a profit, you then have to pay taxes. It is essential that you keep a track of the money going in and out of the company and keep accurate records of every transaction.

▶ **To enjoy a glass of Coke in Asa Candler's day, consumers had to go to a soda fountain. There syrup and soda were mixed and dispensed on the spot.**

From barrel to bottle

Candler's company shipped Coca-Cola syrup to soda fountains all over the United States. The syrup was mixed with soda on the spot. Candler failed to realize that there was a more effective way of selling Coke.

Bottled Coke

Joseph A. Biedenharn, a young merchant from Vicksburg, Mississippi, was the first person to sell Coca-Cola, ready mixed with soda, in a bottle. In 1894 he set up a bottling plant at the back of his drugstore. He wrote to Candler and told him how he sold bottled Coke to the thirsty plantation workers on the Mississippi River. But Candler was not

▲ In 1900 retailers of Coca-Cola bought syrup in pots like this, complete with dispensing instructions on the label.

▶ This elegant opera singer appears on one of the first advertisements for Coca-Cola in bottles – still priced at only five cents.

BUSINESS MATTERS: THE ENTREPRENEUR

An entrepreneur is a business owner or manager who recognizes and exploits new opportunities, and in doing so is prepared to take a risk. Entrepreneurs often invest in untried or original projects in the hope of making a large profit before anyone else gets a chance. They may not create the product or service but recognize its potential. Thomas, Whitehead and Lupton were typical entrepreneurs. They recognized a sound product and grasped the opportunity of distributing it in a more effective way.

▲ Workers in an early bottling plant. Most plants operated only during the summer when demand for soft drinks was highest.

impressed. He failed to see that bottling the drink could boost his sales dramatically and so he missed a vital business opportunity.

The bottling business

Biedenharn, perhaps discouraged by Candler, never extended his business beyond Mississippi. Two young lawyers from Chattanooga, Tennessee, were the first to seize the really rich rewards of bottling. In June 1899 Benjamin F. Thomas and Joseph P. Whitehead applied to Candler for an exclusive contract for bottling Coca-Cola throughout practically the whole of the United States. According to one account, Candler let them have the licence for a dollar.

With John T. Lupton, another Chattanoogan, the two set up bottling plants in Chattanooga and Atlanta. They did not have enough money to open plants nationwide, so they sold franchises elsewhere. In exchange for the name and know-how, local business people paid for the right to bottle and sell Coke in their area.

Within twenty years, there were a thousand bottling plants. In 1928 the sales of bottled Coke overtook sales at soda fountains for the first time. Today you can buy Coke anywhere in a cup or glass or in a variety of glass or plastic bottles and in tin cans. The franchise system is still used by Coca-Cola on a vast international scale.

BUSINESS MATTERS: FRANCHISING

A franchise is an agreement whereby a company such as Coca-Cola (the franchisor) grants a buyer (the franchisee) the right to manufacture and sell its product or service in a certain area for a certain time. The franchisee pays a fee and often a percentage of profits to the franchisor. In return the franchisor offers training, equipment, advertising, perhaps financial help – and most important its name. The franchisee undertakes to maintain the franchisor's standards. Many fast-food chains, such as McDonald's and Burger King, operate on a franchise system. Consumers feel safer with brand names they know. If they have a choice, they usually prefer the familiar to the unknown.

▲ For a while Coke was sold in an all-purpose bottle (centre), used for any drink. Until 1916 bottles (left) had straight sides. Then the classic curved Coke bottle (right) was introduced and has been in use ever since.

The Coca-Cola network

The franchise business is strictly controlled by Coca-Cola. The company ships syrup or concentrate to the bottling plants. The franchisees mix it with sugar and local water, and carbonate it. The water is purified to the highest standards using equipment specified by Coca-Cola. Samples are taken regularly for chemical analysis, and Coca-Cola staff make frequent spot checks to ensure that plants are maintaining the company's standards of cleanliness and quality. Coca-Cola provides its franchisees with the most up-to-date technology available. Franchisees are happy to pay for this 'state of the art' equipment because they need it to meet the company's exacting standards.

Customer to consumer

Each bottler or canner supplies Coke and other Coca-Cola products to the retail trade. Outlets are supermarkets, sweetshops, restaurants, off-licences, pubs and bars. These outlets often sell Coke from vending machines. The franchisees supply and service coolers, vending machines and dispensing equipment to pubs, clubs and restaurants.

In 1991 the company estimated that it sold six million pieces of sales equipment. A fleet of 115,000 trucks, as well as boats, planes and trains keeps Coke on the move.

THE SECRET FORMULA

The classic Coca-Cola drink consists of water and a mixture of sugar, caramel (which gives it its colour), phosphoric acid (which gives it tartness), caffeine (a mild stimulant that you also get in coffee and tea), and natural flavourings. The proportions of these ingredients in Coca-Cola concentrate are a closely guarded trade secret, though all ingredients comply with the health laws of the countries where it is made and sold.

The exact combination of these flavourings is known mysteriously as 'Seven-X'. The formula lies locked in a bank vault in Atlanta. It is said that only three people on the present staff have seen it.

◀ **With the introduction of coolers, Coca-Cola's franchisees were able to extend their sales to offices and factories as well as traditional outlets.**

▶ **McDonald's is Coca-Cola's biggest customer. It sells only Coca-Cola beverages in its outlets.**

▲ A modern canning plant in Britain where six bottling/ canning plants work night and day to supply Coke directly or indirectly to over 300,000 outlets.

BUSINESS MATTERS: AUTOMATION

Automation in a factory means that machines do as much of the manufacturing process as possible. Advances in modern technology mean that Coca-Cola's bottling plants and canneries are highly automated. The blending of syrup and water, container filling and container washing are done automatically. Returnable bottles are washed and re-used, non-returnables can be recycled. Automation means that people no longer have to do these repetitive, boring jobs. Machines are cheaper, stronger and more reliable. Lower costs enable product prices to be lowered.

▼ Miles and miles of supermarket shelving space is taken up with Coca-Cola products.

Coca-Cola grows

In 1919, a few years after Asa's retirement, the Candler family sold its interest in Coca-Cola for $25 million – not a bad return on Candler's original $2,300. A group of rich investors bought the company. They were led by a banker called Ernest Woodruff. Together they re-formed the company into a new corporation, registered in Delaware, and sold shares to the public at $40 each.

Alcohol ban

It was a good time to buy shares in a soft-drinks company. In 1919 the US government banned the manufacture and sale of alcoholic drinks. This ban became known as prohibition and it lasted until 1933. Sales of Coca-Cola, already topping 70 million litres, continued to soar.

▲ Robert Winship Woodruff (1890-1985) was head of Coca-Cola for three decades (1923-1955). He personally took charge of Coca-Cola's marketing strategy, advertising and expansion.

BUSINESS MATTERS: GROWTH AND CASH FLOW

All companies want to grow and make more profits. Knowing when to expand and by how much is tricky. Firms that grow too slowly miss out on profits. Firms that grow too quickly often have to finance their growth by borrowing. This is expensive and often leads to cash-flow problems. They fail to generate enough business to repay their debts and the company has to cease trading. Accountants always keep watch on the company's cash flow, the movement of money in and out of the company.

Recipe for growth

In 1923 Ernest Woodruff's son Robert became president of the company. His guiding principles for the firm were:

Complete loyalty to the company and product.
Simplicity of product (one drink, one bottle, one price).
A good salary for the partners.

Woodruff was full of ideas and energy. He wanted Coca-Cola to be 'within an arm's reach of desire'. He introduced the six-pack carton and the cooler, and in the 1940s, broke his own rule by introducing cans. In 1926 he set up the Foreign Department of Coca-Cola which in 1930 became The Coca-Cola Export Corporation, a subsidiary of the company. It oversaw the setting up of bottling plants all over the world and the distribution of sales equipment.

▲ Before people had cars, carrying home shopping was often a hard job. Easy-to-carry cartons, introduced in 1923, made the task easier.

▶ Robert Woodruff was a stickler for quality in both the product and its image.

GOING GLOBAL

1900-1920 Bottling plants set up all over the US and in Cuba, Guam, Puerto Rico and the Philippines.
1920 First European bottling plant opened in France.
1938 First Australian bottling plant set up in Sydney.

◀ Mexican bottlers proudly display their product. By 1929 Mexico had 10 bottling plants.

▶ 'Within an arm's reach of desire', Coke was made readily available at sports events.

BUSINESS MATTERS: STOCKS AND SHARES

Some companies are privately owned. Others are publicly owned. Often a company decides to 'go public' when it wants to raise money. It offers the public shares in the ownership of the company. Shares are just what they sound like – a share of a company. Together the shares are called stock. Selling stocks and shares is a good way of raising money for expansion but it means that the original owners no longer own the whole company. The board of directors has control and they report to the shareholders. Each year the directors declare a dividend, a sum of money to be divided up among the shareholders as a return on the money they have invested. The amount takes into account the profit made and the amount of money that must be retained for future development. In 1919 The Coca-Cola Company offered 500,000 shares to the public at a price of $40 each, which brought in a total of $20 million. A single share bought at the time would now be worth $20,000.

▲ Coca-Cola is probably a more powerful symbol of the United States than the 'stars-and-stripes' flag. In times of conflict, its advertising has always symbolised friendship.

Coca-Cola and America

Robert Woodruff's three decades in control of Coca-Cola spanned the difficult years of World War II. Before the war Coke was bottled and sold in countries on both sides of the conflict but Woodruff made a point of supporting US troops. Metal cans were introduced to meet their needs. In 1941, when the United States entered the war, Woodruff quickly decided that Coca-Cola's place was near the front line. He sent an order to all staff to 'see that every man in uniform gets a bottle of Coca-Cola for five cents wherever he is and whatever it costs the company'.

The war effort

On 29 June 1943 General Dwight D Eisenhower ordered three million bottles of Coca-Cola to be sent to the Allies in North Africa. Plant and machinery for ten bottling plants were also to be sent so that three million more bottles could be supplied to troops every six months. Coca-Cola sent its top engineers to set up the factories, and in due course there were 64 bottling operations near combat zones in Europe and the Pacific. By the end of hostilities five billion bottles or cans of Coca-Cola had been drunk.

Coca-Cola had not only lifted the spirits of the US armed forces. It had also introduced itself to new markets. When the war ended the bottling plants, and a little bit of America, stayed too.

BUSINESS MATTERS: POLITICS

Working for the government is often beneficial but can also be risky. Some governments try to help businesses by giving them financial help when they are in trouble. They subsidise them in the hope of retaining jobs and their country's share of a particular world market. Other governments believe in a free market. Businesses should make their own way. If they cannot make a profit, they should not be in business.

▶ American troops in World War II experienced many hardships, but they did not have to go without their Coke – still for the price of five cents.

▲ Wartime advertisements showed Coke as the loyal friend of the courageous fighting man.

BUSINESS MATTERS: PUBLICITY

Companies pay for design, advertising and promotional items, but they can also promote their product without paying by attracting publicity from newspapers, magazines and other media. Stories about the company or the product, even if adverse, keep the product in the customers' minds.

The peace effort

When Eisenhower became president of the United States in 1953, he remembered Coca-Cola's response to his call. He rewarded the company with a contract to supply soft drinks at all White House banquets. President John F. Kennedy enjoyed the drink, as did President Jimmy Carter, who like Coca-Cola itself was born in Georgia. Carter used his influence to help Coca-Cola break into the difficult market of communist China.

Friends and foes

Enjoying friendly relations with the US government has not always benefited Coca-Cola. Following the 1967 war between Israel and its Arab neighbours, Coca-Cola was banned for a time from Arab countries. It was also banned in Cuba. It has since been introduced into most Middle East countries, and was served at the Arab-Israeli peace talks in 1993.

▲ Although cans were used during the war years, it was not until 1960 that they were introduced for ordinary consumers.

Branching out

All businesses have to change. They have to keep up with changes going on around them. They have to give their customers something new. They have to fight competition. Despite its enormous success, Coca-Cola was and is no exception to this rule. It has always had fierce competition.

After World War II people had more money and more spare time. They wanted fun and they wanted more things to buy. The Pepsi-Cola Company (now called PepsiCo) was selling its rival drink in a 'maxi-package'. And it had already attracted on to its staff one of Coca-Cola's senior executives. Coke's 'one bottle' of the 1940s rapidly gave place to a variety of bottle sizes. In 1960 came metal cans (which had been introduced during the war) and then, in 1977, family-sized plastic bottles.

NEW PRODUCTS

* Fanta – a range of fizzy drinks with a variety of flavours – was originally made in Germany. It is now the world's third best-selling soft drink.
* Minute Maid – following a merger with Minute Maid Corporation in 1960, Coca-Cola added orange and lemon drinks to its product list, selling under such names as Hi-C, Five-Alive and Bright and Early.
* Tea and coffee – added to Coca-Cola's range in 1960, but since discontinued.
* Wine – added to Coca-Cola's range in 1977, but since discontinued.
* Sprite – a lemon-lime fizzy drink introduced in 1961.
* TAB – Coca-Cola's first low-calorie drink introduced in 1963.
* Fresca – another low-calorie

▼ Just some of The Coca-Cola Company's array of products.

More products

Changing shapes and sizes was not enough. To stay ahead of the competition and please its customers, Coca-Cola had to increase its range of products. During the 1950s and 1960s, it introduced Fanta (which had been invented in Germany in 1940) and several other new drinks, and expanded into new areas of the food business. By doing so it managed to maintain its place as the world's leading seller of soft drinks.

In the 1970s Pepsi-Cola moved into sports goods and in 1977 bought the Pizza-Hut fast-food chain. This turned out to be very profitable, in itself and as an outlet for Pepsi. Coca-Cola was not tempted to stray from its core businesses until 1982. In that year it bought Columbia Pictures, makers and distributors of films and television programmes. With the market in cable television and home videos growing, it proved a good investment.

▲ **Coca-Cola staged a blockbuster promotion for the film *Ghostbusters*.**

fruit drink introduced in 1966.

* Mello Yello – a sugar-citrus drink introduced in 1979.
* Caffeine-free Coke – introduced in 1982.
* diet Coke – a low-calorie cola, called Coca-Cola Light in some countries, introduced in 1982.
* Cherry Coke – a cherry-flavoured variation of Coke introduced in 1982.
* TAB Clear – a sugar-free, calorie-free, colourless but flavourful, cola introduced in 1992.
* PowerAde – a non-carbonated thirst quencher that was the official sports drink of the World Cup 1994 and Olympic Games 1996.
* Nestea – a ready-to-drink tea introduced jointly with Nestlé in 1993.
* Nordic Mist – sparkling water with natural flavours, no caffeine and low sodium introduced in 1993.

BUSINESS MATTERS: DIVERSIFICATION

There is a limit to the amount anyone can sell of a single product. Businesses need to expand and often they do so by creating new products or buying other companies to acquire ready-made new products. The widening of a range of business activities is called diversification. Having a range of products helps to spread risk. If one product is doing badly, another might be doing well. In a wet summer ice cream might sell slowly, umbrellas fast. One danger of diversification is that buying into different businesses is expensive. You may have to borrow the money and get into debt in order to keep going, and the new product may not live up to expectations.

Coke old and new

▲ Roberto Goizueta (born 1933) began work for Coca-Cola in Havana in 1954. He became chairman and chief executive in 1981, and has been responsible for the company's continuing growth and diversification.

The person who masterminded the introduction of new products during the 1980s and took the bold step of buying Columbia Pictures was chairman Roberto Goizueta. In 1982, responding to public demand for a low-calorie cola, Coca-Cola had successfully introduced diet Coke. In 1984, however, Goizueta became alarmed. Coca-Cola's total share of the soft-drinks market fell for the first time ever, and Pepsi's sales rose. The difference was only slight but it was clear evidence that young people were turning from Coke to Pepsi.

Secret survey

During experiments to develop diet Coke the company had come up with an alternative recipe for regular Coke – a new taste in the bottle or can. Perhaps this would reverse the trend. The new drink was blind-tested alongside the old one by a sample of 190,000 people aged between 13 and 59. (In a blind test neither product is identified.) Of the sample, 61 per cent said they preferred the new taste to the old.

Out with the old, in with the new

In April 1985 Coca-Cola announced that the 99-year-old Pemberton formula was to abandoned. At the end of the summer the old Coke would disappear for good. This was a bombshell to bottlers, canners and consumers. Millions of Americans rushed to try the new Coke, and sales rocketed.

▼ 1982 was a big year for Coca-Cola. It bought Columbia Pictures and introduced several new products, including diet Coke, sales of which have steadily increased over the years.

BUSINESS MATTERS: CHOICE

Often shoppers are dazzled by the choice before them in a well-stocked supermarket. Which washing powder should they choose? Which make of beans? Price, design, familiarity are all factors that influence the customer's choice. Customers are often loyal to products, but some also like a change. Successful businesses balance these twin demands. They strive to make sure that they have better products than their competitors, give better value for money, and make their products stand out among the rest in the market-place. Coca-Cola has managed to increase the numbers of loyal consumers. They mostly like the taste to stay the same, but enjoy occasional new packaging and new containers. They also like a choice between Coke with caffeine or without, with sugar or without, can or bottle and so on.

But for many, the new Coke tasted too sweet and was not fizzy enough. People complained. A television station commissioned a public opinion poll. Of those sampled, 59 per cent preferred the old Coke, 25 per cent preferred Pepsi and 13 per cent new Coke.

Bowing to the public

In spite of all their careful and costly market research, the new formula was not an outright winner. In July 1985 Goizueta made an announcement. Coca-Cola would bow to public opinion. The old formula would not die. It would live on as Coca-Cola Classic alongside the new Coke. Goizueta had by chance introduced a new product and boosted flagging sales of an old one. People did not want one product or the other; they wanted a choice.

BUSINESS MATTERS: MARKET RESEARCH

When John Pemberton made his historic march to Jacobs' Pharmacy, he was intent on conducting market research. In the past businesses used to launch products on a hunch – some, such as publishers, still do. But most successful businesses would not dream of launching a product without finding out if it suited their intended customers – the target market. They can commission surveys of consumer demands and preferences, test an experimental version of their product and make sales forecasts. Often business people can predict the results of the research. They know from experience what the market wants. But they are not always right, and nor is the research.

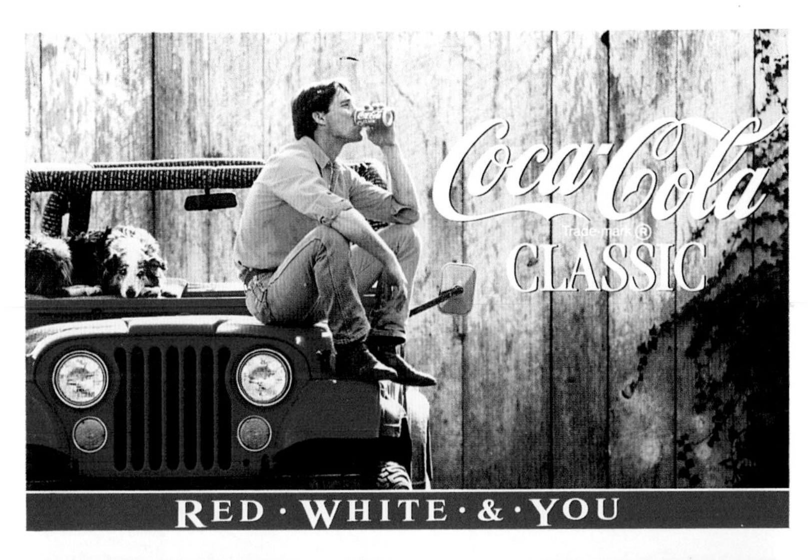

◀ Old Coke or new? For those who like change, there is a fast bike and a wave to catch, for those who don't, there is a solid dependable car and man's best friend.

Working for Coca-Cola

Some 32,000 people work directly for Coca-Cola and about another 650,000 indirectly. The company fosters a spirit of community in its workers. They like to think that they share a common culture even though they are spread through 195 countries. Loyalty to the product has always been instilled into the workforce who are encouraged to take pride in the quality of all Coca-Cola products.

Because bottling and canning are now highly automated Coca-Cola and its franchisees employ far fewer unskilled workers than in the past. Today the workers in a bottling plant are there to keep an eye on the conveyor belts, to monitor the machinery or analyse the water and the syrup, or

▲ Trainee managers undertake courses designed to develop leadership and decision-making skills.

▶ You never see a dirty Coca-Cola truck on the roads. This driver and his truck reinforce Coca-Cola's clean and wholesome image.

to help keep the factory scrupulously clean. Others, inside and out, load and drive the trucks for distribution.

As well as the production and distribution staff, Coca-Cola and its trading partners employ sales and marketing people, chemists, accountants, computer experts, managers, directors and all kinds of office staff.

Staff benefits

Coca-Cola makes a point of staff training, mostly on the job, in its own premises. It likes its staff to work in pleasant surroundings and to feel that they could not do better elsewhere. To attract and retain talented people it pays competitive wages and salaries and offers attractive benefits, such as pension and profit-sharing schemes.

BUSINESS MATTERS: HUMAN RESOURCES

The people who work for a company are its most important asset. They are also its most expensive. Highly talented people are hard to come by and rival firms are always ready to poach staff. So businesses have to pay as well as they can. Lower down the scale, where jobs demand fewer skills, more workers are available, so salaries and wages are not so high. When companies need to make economies, they lay off (mostly junior) staff. In many countries they have to pay considerable compensation, but even so it is cheaper to make workers redundant than to keep them on and wait for better times.

◀ A tiny proportion of Coca-Cola's staff is based at the headquarters in Atlanta. Thousands more work in places far away where Coke is virtually the only link with America.

How Coke manages

The people who own Coca-Cola are its shareholders. The board of directors is answerable to them. If the company makes a good profit the shareholders will benefit. If it makes a loss the value of the shares will fall and so will the shareholders' faith in the company's directors.

The board of directors

As in all large companies, the top decisions in Coca-Cola are made by the board of directors. The Coca-Cola Company's Board of Directors has 14 members. Of these some are executive directors who work full-time for Coca-Cola. The others are non-executive directors.

The chairman of the board supervises its meetings and ensures that its decisions are carried out by the company. Carrying out the decisions is primarily the job of the chief executive. At Coca-Cola, as in many other companies, the

BUSINESS MATTERS: DIRECTORS

As well as the executive directors who run the business, every large company has non-executive directors. These are distinguished executives from other large companies, such as banks, financial institutions, airlines, insurance firms or other industries. They lend their expertise to the executive directors and help them make decisions by offering unbiased advice. It is also their job to make sure that the executive directors are up to scratch. It would be difficult for junior members of a board to oust an incompetent or corrupt chief executive – their boss – without the help of the non-executive directors. So the role of the non-executive director is an important one.

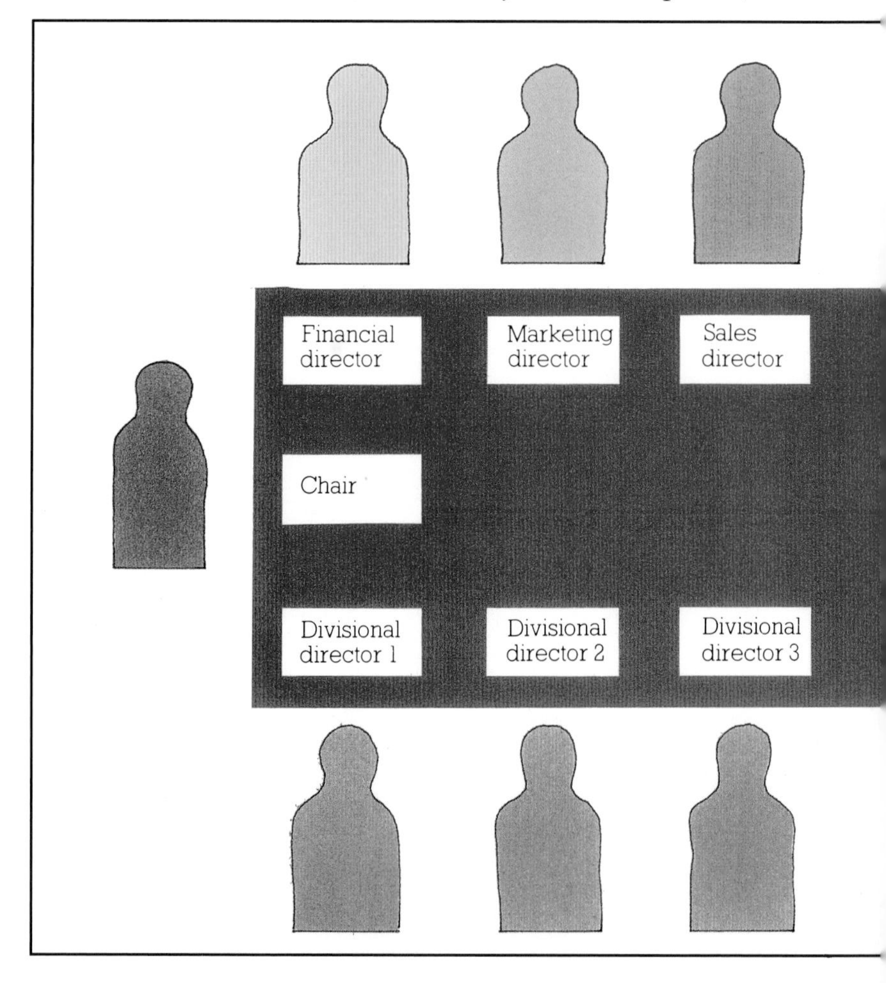

▶ **A typical board of directors of a large company. In smaller companies directors may have more than one role. In very small companies there may be only one director.**

position of chairman and chief executive are held by one person.

The corporate officers

The chairman delegates responsibility either to the other directors or to the corporate officers who control various divisions of the company. Corporate officers include a chief financial officer, a treasurer, a company secretary, a general counsel (lawyer) and a large number of senior vice-presidents and vice-presidents. Many serve on sub-committees to the board.

Divisions and subsidiaries

Coca-Cola has five operating groups. Between them they control and keep in touch with the global network of bottlers, canners, distributors and sales forces. In addition there is The Minute Maid Company, a wholly-owned subsidiary based in Houston, Texas.

BUSINESS MATTERS: MANAGEMENT

At every level of a company it is important for people to work as efficiently as possible. Managers have the job of seeing that they do. It is their role to enable their staff to carry out their work efficiently, cost effectively and on time. They have to make sure that employees are confident and happy in their work and feel well rewarded and keen for promotion. No matter how good the workers are, they cannot perform well with a poor management that lacks direction and drive, or fails to understand the workers' problems.

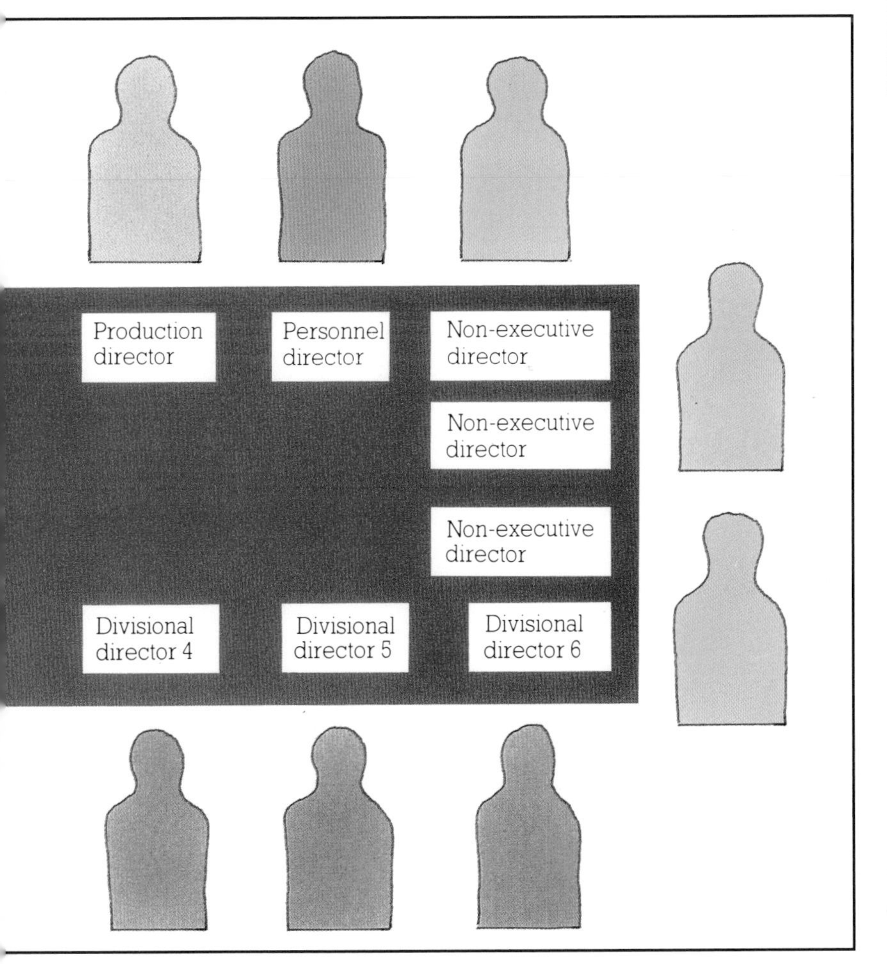

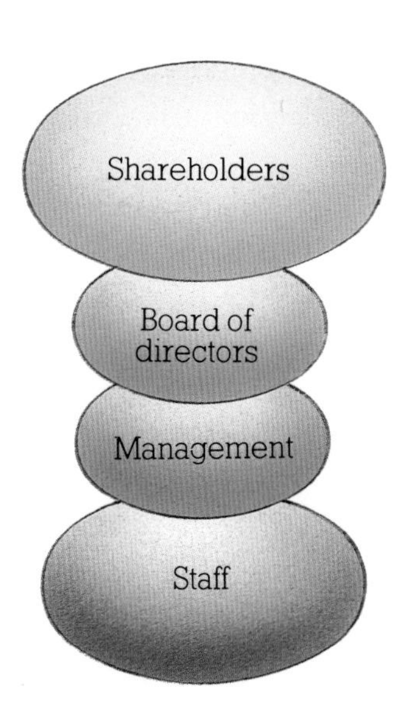

▲ **The board of directors is answerable to the shareholders. The management and staff are answerable to the board.**

The system

If you ask most business people to describe their business structure, they compare it to a pyramid. At the peak is the chairman or chairwoman, beneath him or her the board, beneath them the managers, beneath them the workers and at the base the customers and consumers. The Coca-Cola Company describes its business as a pyramid, but an inverted one – with the six billion all-important consumers at the top.

The diagram shows the size and scope of the Coca-Cola system at the present time. By the time you read this, the pyramid will probably have grown broader and stronger.

▼ Coca-Cola already has 6 billion consumers. Ads like this one seek to broaden Coke's appeal to older, more sophisticated people.

Consumers
6 billion thirsty people consume products at a rate of 834 million a day

Sales Equipment
6 million pieces, including 2 million vending machines

Marketing and Advertising
20 million pieces, costing $4 billion

Customers
8 million, creating $66 billion retail sales

Production and Distribution
13 billion cases (24 bottles or cans), delivered by 115,000 vehicles

People
650,000 (including those of franchises) paid $8 billion in wages

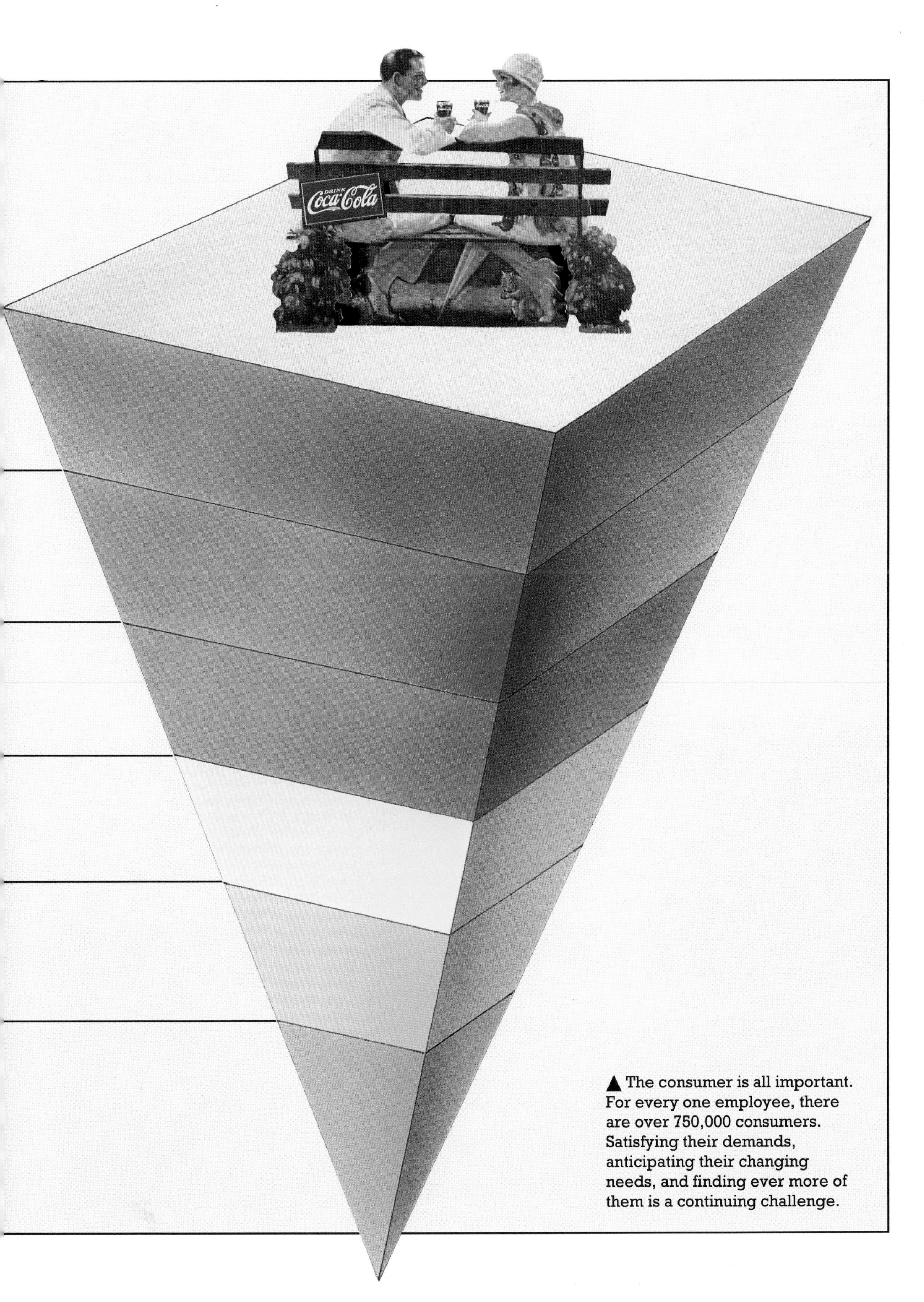

▲ The consumer is all important. For every one employee, there are over 750,000 consumers. Satisfying their demands, anticipating their changing needs, and finding ever more of them is a continuing challenge.

▲ An elegant appeal to sportsmen and spectators in 1948.

Advertising Coke

Coca-Cola and its sister products outsell their nearest rival by about two to one. One of the main reasons for this is Coca-Cola's advertising. The company spends millions on advertising each year. Its campaigns are legendary.

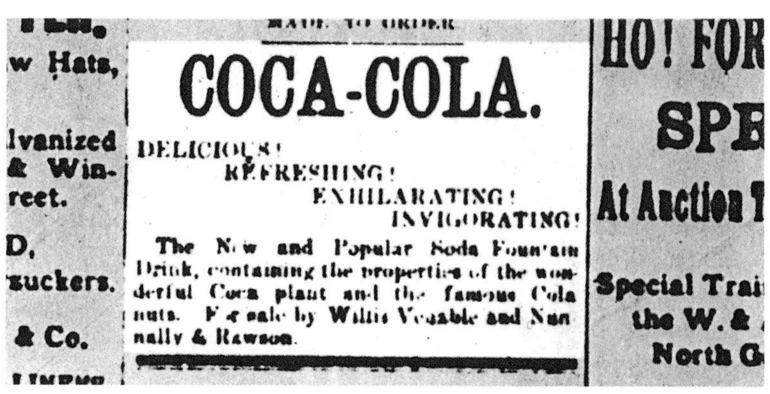

COCA-COLA.

DELICIOUS! REFRESHING! EXHILARATING! INVIGORATING!

The New and Popular Soda Fountain Drink, containing the properties of the wonderful Coca plant and the famous Cola nuts. For sale by Willis Venable and Nunnally & Rawson.

▶ The first ever newspaper advertisement for Coca-Cola appeared in the *Atlanta Journal* on 29 May 1886. It was not Coke's snappiest slogan ever!

▼ Coca-Cola sponsored an early television show featuring Edgar Bergen and sidekick Charlie McCarthy.

John Pemberton, the inventor of Coca-Cola, was the first to advertise it. In the *Atlanta Journal* of 29 May 1886, he extolled it as 'Delicious! Refreshing! Exhilarating! Invigorating!' Today a typical advertisement shows young people relaxing with friends and a convivial Coke – with the Coca-Cola logo much in evidence. Snappier slogans are carefully worded for maximum memorability and impact.

▶ The message is the same whatever language it comes in. This is a 1940s advertisement from Greece.

▼ Coca-Cola swings in the 1960s, with 'Things Go Better With Coke'.

SLOGANS

* The Pause That Refreshes (1929)
* It's The Refreshing Thing to Do (1936)
* Its The Real Thing (1942 and revived in 1969)
* Global High Sign (1944)
* Things Go Better With Coke (1963)
* Have A Coke And A Smile (1979)
* Coke Is It (1982)
* You Can't Beat The Feeling (1987)
* Always (1993).

Selling the world

Cinema and television advertising is especially important to Coca-Cola. One commercial stands out as a classic. It was screened in 1971 when the Vietnam War was still raging and the Cold War between East and West was as icy as ever. In the advertisement a vast crowd of young men and women gather on a hilltop and sing 'I'd like to buy the world a Coke'. It summed up Coca-Cola's message – refreshment, youthfulness, universal friendship.

▲ Images of friendship and togetherness, brought about by Coke featured in 1971's 'It's The Real Thing' campaign.

Advertising agency

Coca-Cola uses a number of top international agencies, to create and carry out many of its campaigns. It is up to them and other such advisers to catch the mood of the moment and keep in touch with the mind of the market. In 1985 the agency prepared the campaign for the new Coke. It produced two slogans. One, 'Catch The Wave', sought to catch the young. The other, 'Red, White & You', sought to hold the loyalty of established customers.

◀ Youth, equality and friendship is the message of the 1976 'Coke Adds Life' campaign.

▲ The Coca-Cola Sprite was created during the war years. The ever smiling boy glowed with optimism.

Coke's image

Anyone who wants to sell a new product needs to make the public aware of it and promote it. A product must have an image. This image is created by advertising and by the way the product is 'dressed' and presented to the public.

Designed for sales

Consciously or unconsciously we all make choices about design. Coca-Cola's red and white labels with the 'dynamic curve' based on accountant Robinson's script are extremely distinctive. The elegant shape of the Coke bottle is as legendary as some Coca-Cola advertising. Cans and plastic bottles may be more convenient but the classic Coke bottle has a seemingly undying appeal. It looks attractive and is easy to hold.

Making the product look attractive and instantly recognizable is part of any company's overall marketing strategy. Packaging and point-of-sales material must grab the

BUSINESS MATTERS: MERCHANDISING

Merchandising refers to the whole process of selling merchandise or goods, but it has two more specialized meanings too. The production of novelty items to be given away as gifts to promote another product, such as paper hats to promote hamburgers, is also called merchandising. So is the sale of the right to use a company's logo or livery on goods for sale. Some companies with a distinctive trademark or character make a lot of money from licensing their use. The Disney Corporation sells Mickey Mouse ears, clocks, hats and all kinds of novelties. It also sells the rights for others to use its characters. If you wanted to put Mickey Mouse on a T-shirt you would have to have permission and you would have to pay the Disney Corporation for the privilege.

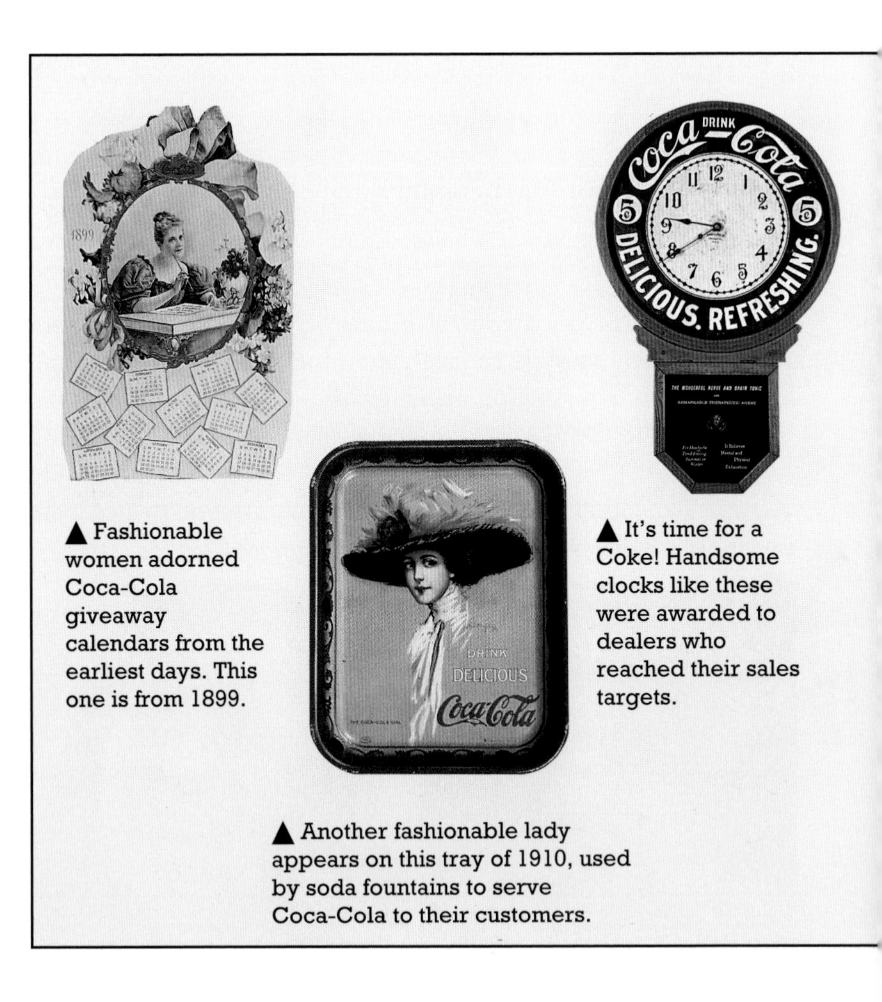

▲ Fashionable women adorned Coca-Cola giveaway calendars from the earliest days. This one is from 1899.

▲ Another fashionable lady appears on this tray of 1910, used by soda fountains to serve Coca-Cola to their customers.

▲ It's time for a Coke! Handsome clocks like these were awarded to dealers who reached their sales targets.

customer's attention. It must stand out from other products on the supermarket shelves. Since Coca-Cola has many different products competing with each other, it is important that each brand has a look as distinct as its flavour.

▲ Not just a star of the opera, Lillian Nordica's image appeared on items as diverse as menus and huge metal signs between 1903 and 1905.

Promotional items

The words 'free gift' are one of the best selling tools. As early as 1888 Asa Candler sought to boost sales by giving incentives to his dealers. Those who achieved high sales levels might win a special syrup urn.

From 1900 bottlers also gave desirable prizes to customers, and small gifts, such as razor blades and chewing gum, to the public. The gifts were useful to the recipients and to the company, since they carried the company logo and reminded people of the product. Since the early days more and more items have been designed as giveaways. These are now strictly controlled by Coca-Cola. An official merchandise licensing programme ensures that all gifts or products that bear the Coca-Cola logo meet with their approval.

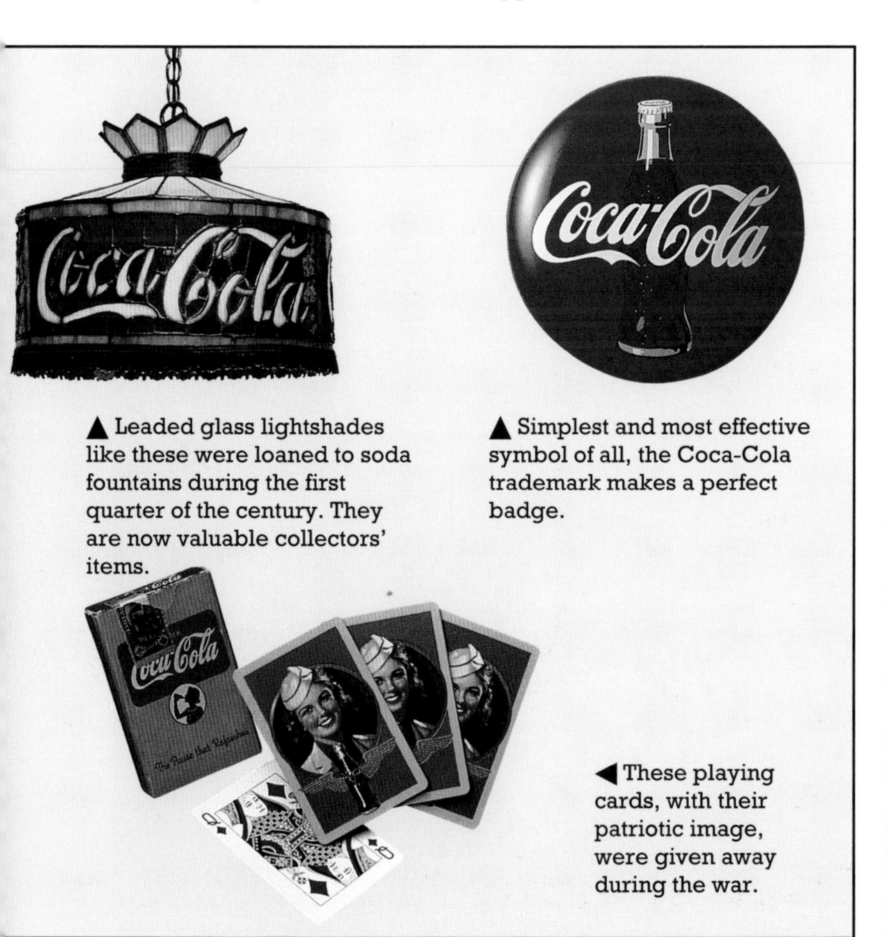

▲ Leaded glass lightshades like these were loaned to soda fountains during the first quarter of the century. They are now valuable collectors' items.

▲ Simplest and most effective symbol of all, the Coca-Cola trademark makes a perfect badge.

◀ These playing cards, with their patriotic image, were given away during the war.

COLLECTING COCABILIA

Since the 1890s a bewildering array of objects decked in Coke colours and adorned with its logo have been created: glass lamps and ornaments, calendars, cigar-bands, coasters, clocks, schoolbooks and bags, matchbooks, notepads, paper napkins, paperweights, pencils and pencil sharpeners, playing cards, posters, thermometers, tea trays . . . Many items are in The World of Coca-Cola museum in Atlanta. Others are in private collections. Some are quite valuable and rare. But, beware, there are a lot of counterfeit copies in circulation.

Protecting Coke's image

Anyone with a successful product needs to prevent other people from copying it. Inventors apply for a patent for their inventions and traders register trademarks. Once a product has a trademark, nobody else may use it or its name. Like many other companies, Coca-Cola uses its name as a logo (short for logogram).

BRAND IMAGE

A survey carried out in 11 countries in 1990 indicated that, out of 6,000 brands tested, Coca-Cola was the most powerful and successful brand name in the world. (McDonald's came eighth, and Pepsi tenth).

Copying Coke

On 31 January 1893 Asa Candler registered the Coca-Cola logo as a trademark with the United States Patents and

▼ The Coke bottle and its contents have been successful for more than 80 years. Stamping out substitute brews, imitation bottles and fake labels has kept investigators and lawyers busy. The bottle itself was registered as a trademark in 1977.

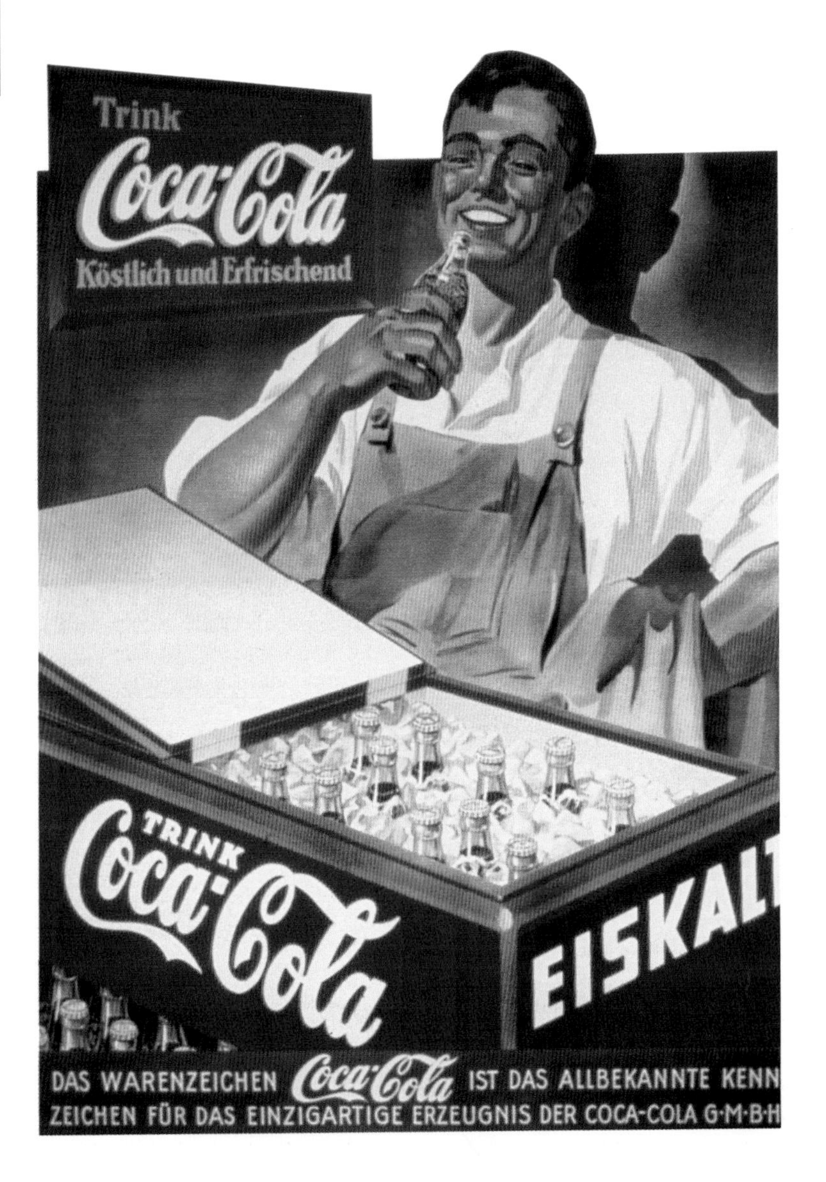

▶ This German advertisement makes the point. The warning in black and white is almost as large as the 'Delicious and Refreshing' slogan.

◀ Outlets that sell other kinds of cola often serve up their own brand when asked for Coca-Cola, a practice that Coca-Cola has always tried to stop.

Trademarks Office. It was the first crucial step in protecting The Coca-Cola Company's most precious asset after its formula – its brand name. Coca-Cola quickly became popular and had many imitators, and counterfeiters who were dishonest enough to use the Coca-Cola logo on their products.

The logo is an irreplaceable part of the company's image. If it or the secret formula were to become public property, Coca-Cola would lose its identity. In 1967 the trademark was valued by experts at $3 billion. No wonder the company spends thousands of dollars to protect it.

It took a long time before Coca-Cola was successful in registering its short name Coke. It failed completely to register the word cola which can now be used by anybody to describe a sweet caramel-coloured drink.

The Coca-Cola Company vigorously protects all its trademarks – including Fanta, Sprite and the rest. Nobody may use them without first seeking the company's approval.

THE WRATH OF COKE

The Coca-Cola Company battled to establish its right to the name Cola, but the courts would not agree. So cola went the way of aspirin and nylon, which are considered ordinary words spelled with lower-case letters, though they too were once trademarks. The author John Steinbeck made the mistake of using the word coke (without a capital) in his novel *The Wayward Bus.* Worse, he implied that the drink was the same as Pepsi. As a result Coca-Cola published a set of guidelines for its own advertisers, as well as for writers and journalists, that are still in use today. If the rules are broken, Coca-Cola can sue for compensation.

BUSINESS MATTERS: TRADEMARKS AND PATENTS

A trademark, also called a brand name, is a name, a design, a symbol, an object, or a sound that distinguishes one company's products from another. Because a trademark represents a company's reputation, it is carefully guarded. A company like Coca-Cola would never allow its logo to be used on anything that it was not proud to be associated with.

Patents are official government documents that establish an individual's or company's exclusive right, or title, to an invention for a certain period. An invention can include anything designed, created or made up, so trademarks, like any other inventions can be protected by patents. Unauthorised use of a patented trademark can lead to prosecution.

The cola wars

As soon as it became successful Coca-Cola was imitated. Lookalike drinks appeared with brand names like Cola Nova, Cola Sola, Better Cola, and even Cola Kola. Most quickly disappeared but one survived to become Coke's main rival – Pepsi-Cola.

Coke's rival

Pepsi-Cola has fought a long war with Coca-Cola for the bulk of the world's soft-drinks markets. Coca-Cola has long been the market leader in Australia, Canada, Germany, Italy,

◀ PepsiCo aims its advertising at exactly the same market – everyone – as Coca-Cola. Here the appeal is to the young vigorous strong man.

BUSINESS MATTERS: COMPETITION

Competition in business is the struggle for customers and profits between two or more enterprises in the same field. People who believe in a free market support competition: it forces up standards, as competitors seek to outdo each other in product quality and business efficiency. It also keeps prices down. Without competition businesses can charge what they like. In the former Soviet Union and other communist countries, all industries were state controlled. There was no competition and as a result most factories and businesses were hopelessly outdated and inefficient. The system however did mean that there was full employment. Nowadays workers are being laid off, just as they are in developed countries when enterprises reorganize, contract or go out of business.

Japan and Latin America. Pepsi-Cola has carved out markets in parts of Africa, Central and Eastern Europe, and the Middle East. Coke has overtaken Pepsi in Russia but the two still battle it out elsewhere in Europe, in the United States and China. In 1985 both went into space aboard a NASA space shuttle.

Competition hots up

Before and during World War II, Coca-Cola had little to fear from Pepsi-Cola. Then, in 1949, Alfred N. Steele, a top executive with Coca-Cola, was enticed into becoming head of Pepsi-Cola. Steele turned Pepsi's fortunes. He introduced larger bottle sizes, different packaging and invested in a massive advertising campaign. Net earnings went up by 1000 per cent. Coca-Cola had to respond to the challenge. It repackaged Coke and introduced new bottle sizes.

Answering Pepsi-Cola's challenge

In the 1970s Pepsi-Cola devised an original and effective campaign. They issued the 'Pepsi Challenge'. They asked people to compare the taste of Pepsi and Coke, without knowing which was which. More people preferred the taste of Pepsi, a result that they used to great effect in their advertising. This was not just a gimmick. Coca-Cola carried out the same tests and got the same results. It had not occurred to them to test their product – they 'knew' it was better. Their success had made them complacent and they had to fight hard to maintain their position.

During the 1980s and 1990s Coca-Cola has been kept on its toes by Pepsi-Cola. It has constantly had to combat the youthful image that Pepsi's advertising presents. It has maintained its leadership of the soft-drinks market by concentrating on a narrower range of businesses.

BUSINESS MATTERS: DIRECT COMPETITION

Businesses can compete in various ways. Mostly they try to be at least slightly different from their rivals. They try to offer a better product or service or price or operate in different areas. Direct competition, with two companies offering virtually identical products to the same customers, is rare, especially when one of the rivals is well-established. The rivalry between Coca-Cola and Pepsi-Cola is the most famous example of direct competition in the world. Coca-Cola had a 13-year start on Pepsi but PepsiCo was confident enough to challenge them, and stay at their heels. Their determination to outreach each other has resulted in both companies growing and growing, and ever more cola being drunk. Though Pepsi-Cola is not as big as Coca-Cola, it is highly profitable. Often a brand leader has to spend so much money on staying in the lead that its profits are reduced, and its shareholders make less money.

◀ Colas account for only one third of Pepsi's turnover. The rest comes from its fast-food outlets, such as Pizza Hut and Kentucky Fried Chicken. Both these chains of course sell only PepsiCo soft-drink products, including their new low-calorie cola Pepsi Max.

▲ Since 1928 when Coca-Cola was sold from little huts like this one outside the stadium in Amsterdam, Coca-Cola has always been a major player in the Olympic Games.

Coke in the community

Coca-Cola seeks in its advertising and public relations to promote a positive public image. It is a promoter of refreshment and friendship. It pursues a 'good neighbour' policy in all that it does.

In its home town of Atlanta people have a great affection for the company. When Asa Candler died in 1929, Atlanta declared a day of mourning for him. He had always supported local projects of importance to the community. Streets and squares were named after him and his product.

Sponsorship

Coca-Cola does much at home and abroad to promote its product by supporting good causes. It provides money for sporting and cultural events. In return it gets its name prominently displayed on publicity for the events and at the event itself.

Coke has been involved with the Olympic Games since 1928. The only year in which Coca-Cola was not served to athletes was in 1980 when the United States boycotted the games. The athletes who did compete did not go thirsty, however. They were provided with Fanta.

The environment

Coca-Cola produces mountains of packaging. All of its glass and plastic bottles and its metal cans are recyclable. Most of its literature is produced on recycled paper. It also backs many

▼ In this 1984 advertisement Coke has given itself a gold medal. It has been the official soft drink of the games for nearly 70 years.

projects that encourage people to recycle more of their packaging and rubbish. In the United Kingdom, for example, it supports the Tidy Britain Group in its litter-prevention campaign and was the first major supporter of Save-a-Can. It offers educational packs and computer software to help children learn about the environment and the effect of litter in the community.

▶ **Ring pulls that detach completely from the can are environmentally unfriendly. Coca-Cola cans now have ring pulls that stay put after opening.**

▼ **Schools welcome Coca-Cola's educational material. Children are encouraged to take care of the environment and become aware of Coke products at the same time.**

BUSINESS MATTERS: PROFITS AND TAXES

A business, like an individual, has to pay tax on its income. It can take money out of its earnings to pay for staff wages, office or factory rent, and other business costs and expenses. Anything left over is profit and the business must pay tax on it.

In most countries companies gain certain tax advantages by donating money to charities. This allows them to keep or use more of their profits than they could otherwise and therefore encourages them to continue giving to charity. (It benefits the government, since it would have to pick up the welfare bill if charities did not exist.) Sponsoring a sporting or cultural event or a hospital project helps successful companies use some of their profit in a way that benefits the community. This in turn helps to give the corporation a positive public image and a lot of 'free visibility'.

The future

The brown drink with the refreshing taste and the secret formula, first made in an Atlanta backyard, has travelled all round the world and even been in orbit round it. Coca-Cola's first 100 years have been full of changes. It has proved itself adaptable. It has responded to market changes and new openings.

▲ Despite political differences between the United States and China, sales of Coke go from strength to strength as economic reforms slacken communism's grip of the nation.

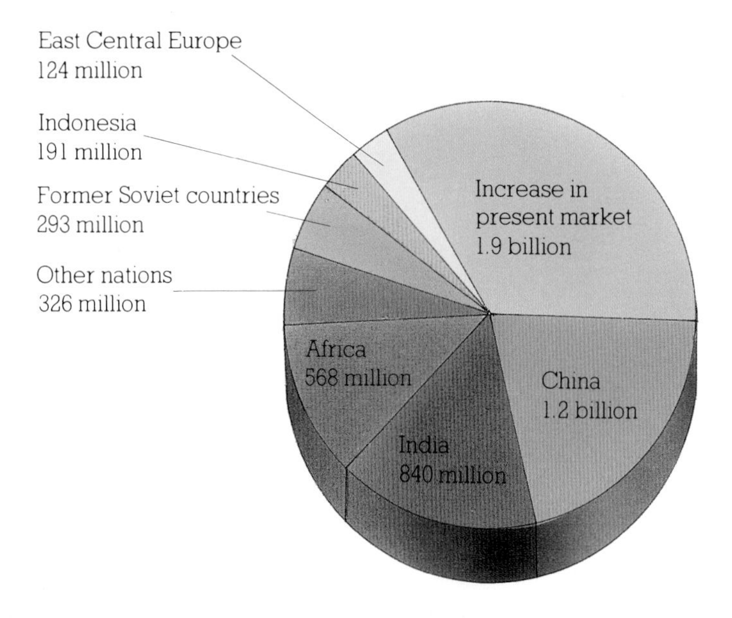

◀ All over the world new markets are opening up to Coca-Cola, many as a result of political changes. Amazing as it may seem, the majority of the world's population are not yet consumers of Coca-Cola. The diagram shows the extent of Coca-Cola's target markets.

Developing new markets

In the last decade of the twentieth century the world is going through a change. Fewer babies are being born in the United States and Europe, but the world's population is still rising. A recent estimate suggests that there will be six billion people living on our planet by the year 2000.

While the proportion of older people in the developed nations is rising, the reverse is happening in less developed areas of the world. In Latin America and southern Asia and the Pacific region, the population of young people is rising rapidly. These areas are also getting richer. Coca-Cola has always appealed to the young, so it seems likely that it will concentrate its marketing efforts in these regions.

Growth of food products

Minute Maid, Coca-Cola's Houston-based food subsidiary – has grown greatly since 1960. In the 1980s it became the leader in new products and packages. In the 1990s it has become the leading manufacturer of orange juice and juice-

▼ TAB Clear is just one of several new products that Coca-Cola has introduced in the last few years, in order to extend its product range and broaden its consumer base.

BUSINESS MATTERS: ALL CHANGE

Everything is always changing. Nothing in business ever stands still. Good managers and business people look to the future. They know that a business is only as good as its people and equipment and their skills. Today technology changes at an amazing speed. Unless businesses keep up with the changes, they can easily be outstripped by their rivals. The Coca-Cola Company's first 100 years were full of changes. It proved adaptable and ready to respond to changes in the market. That is its success. It is now well into its second century, looking forward to new opportunities, and still guarding its precious – unchanging? – secret.

▲ Coca-Cola devised a special can for astronauts to take into space aboard the shuttle. The fizz remained even under zero gravity.

drinks in the United States. It pioneered aseptic (germ-free) packaging for juice drinks. The management sees room for much more growth in these products and a source of future profits. It is also likely to take its business worldwide.

Into space

The future for Coca-Cola seems limitless. Every day applications continue to flood in to run bottling plants – even on the moon. Coke has already been enjoyed in the weightlessness of earth orbit. The company designed the first space container for the shuttle astronauts to drink from. Who knows, Coca-Cola may be the first soft drink to find a home on a new planet.

▼ Coca-Cola rode into space aboard the shuttle (along with Pepsi). Where will it go next? Will it be the first soft drink to land on another planet?

Create your own business

▲ The first step in a business is very important: to think of a good idea for a product or service to offer. What do you think your friends and their parents might pay good money for? Ask them before you spend any money.

Coca-Cola's name is everywhere. By making itself so visible and available Coke sells more and more of its products. It also makes money from merchandise that bears its logo. See if you can raise money for your school or for a charity using your school 'logo' – its badge or motto.

First you must ask permission from the headteacher. He or she controls the rights to the logo and will want to know what kind of items you intend selling. They must be things the school can be proud of.

Many firms specialize in manufacturing items for merchandising. You will find them in the Yellow Pages. The items they produce include gifts of all kinds, pens and pencils, erasers, and clothing such as T-shirts. They also produce novelty items and gadgets such as fridge magnets.

Management
You will need to select or elect a small team to manage your project. Each person must have a specific role – to look after the money, the design, the publicity, the selling and so on.

Capital
For this project, you will need money to start with. If everyone contributes some of their own money, they will find their parents more willing to lend some. You must offer to return their money with interest.

Planning
Decide what you want to do. Do you want to buy a quantity of felt-tip pens with the school's name on them, or do you want to make your own product? Think who you will be selling to. Who are your customers? What will they want? What will be the right price for them? Would they like a school mug? Would they like a pack of greetings cards printed by a local printer? Do some market research.

Estimate the maximum number of items you can sell.

◀ Decide on your product, its price, and how you will promote and sell it. Decide how you will produce it. Who will help you? How much will it cost and how much money will you raise from sales? How much money do you need to start up your business and keep it going? Careful planning will help you avoid mistakes.

What is the minimum? What is the likely number?

Costing

When you have decided what you want to sell, see if it will work financially. How much will you have to pay to produce, pack, advertise and distribute your product? Remember your overheads – the cost of extra items like bus fares, stationery and postage that you will use in your business. How much can you sell for? Work out the cost per item by adding all the costs together and dividing them by the number of items you are purchasing or producing. Work out the amount of money you hope to make if you sell all of your stock, and divide it by the number of items. The difference between the two amounts will be your profit per item. Work out how many items you must sell to cover your costs and get back all the money you have spent. This is your break-even point, anything less and you make a loss, anything more and you make a profit.

Selling

Buy or make your product and drum up publicity for it. Advertise it in the school magazine. Put up home-made posters. Ask a local newspaper to run a story. There should be no need for you to spend money on advertising. Drum up custom by talking to your friends and their parents.

▼ Proper businesses present their figures as a profit and loss account like this.

PROFIT AND LOSS ACCOUNT		
Sales		300.00
Less Cost of sales		
Wool	50.00	
Needles	5.00	
Design	20.00	
	75.00	75.00
Gross profit	225.00	
Less Overheads		
Rent	5.00	
Wages	45.00	
Stationery	5.00	
Hire of bike	10.00	65.00
Net profit		160.00
Loan repayment	100.00	
Interest	10.00	
Net profit after interest		50.00

Accounts

Keep a record of what you spend and what you receive. Repay your investors and give the profit you make to the charity you chose. If you make a lot of money, you may want to reinvest part of it in a more ambitious business project for next year.

The language of business

Accountant Person who keeps or inspects accounts. See also Treasurer.
Accounts Records that show money going in or out of a business.
Advertising Making publicly known. Advertisers use television, radio, newspapers and so on to tell everyone how good their product or service is. See also Promotion.
Analyse To examine something minutely.
Assets Anything owned by a business including property, money, goods and machines.
Automation Manufacture of a product using machines rather than people.
Billion A thousand million or, in Britain, a million million. Billions in this book are a thousand million.
Board of directors See Directors.
Brand The name of a company's product. See also Trademark.
Break-even The point at which income from sales equals the cost of production and sales.
Business An organization that sells goods or services in return for money.
Capital Money needed to start a business and keep it going.
Cash flow The rate at which money enters and leaves a business during any period of time.
Cent See Dollar.
Chairman The person who leads a committee or board of directors. Also called a chairperson or chair.
Chief executive The highest-ranking person in a company who has full power to act and make decisions on behalf of the company.
Choice Variety of products for customers to choose from.
Communism Economic and political system in which the state controls farms, factories and businesses, which are held in common ownership.
Company Organization of a group of people to carry on a business. Companies may be small or large, public or private. See also Corporation.
Company secretary Person who records the meetings and decisions of the board of directors.
Competition The struggle for customers and profits between two or more enterprises in the same field.
Consumer The purchaser or user of an article. See also Customer.
Contract Legal agreement between two or more persons. It can be written or spoken.
Conveyor belt A continuously moving belt which transports goods, materials or packages during manufacture.
Core business The most dependable area of a business that has diverse interests.
Corporate officers Senior managers of a corporation. They include the chief executive officer, the president, the executive officers and vice-presidents. In Britain these officers are usually called directors. See Directors.
Corporation Business corporations are usually large, centrally organized public companies.
Costs The amount of capital that it takes to make and sell a product or service; costings are forecasts of those costs.
Credit To give credit is to allow time for a payment to be made. Bookkeepers write down payments as credits, and debts as debits. A creditor is a person or business to whom a business owes money.
Customer Anyone who buys from a seller, especially one who buys regularly. A customer is not necessarily a consumer. Coca-Cola's customers are retailers. The retailers' customers are consumers.
Debit See Credit.
Directors People who guide the activities of a company and make its most important decisions. They are members of the board of directors, which is led by the chairman or chief executive. See also Corporate officers.
Diversification The widening of the range of goods and services produced.
Dividend A small part of a company's profits paid to a shareholder in return for his or her investment.
Dollar Unit of US currency made up of 100 cents. The equivalent in UK pounds at the moment is about 66 pence, but rates of exchange between countries vary all the time.
Drugstore Shops in the US that sell soft drinks, snacks, sweets, cosmetics and over-the-counter medicines.
Earnings Money gained by a person working or by a company selling.
Economy 1 Careful use of resources or reductions in costs. 2 Overall administration of a community's or country's resources.
Enterprise 1 A business or company. 2 Originality and inventiveness shown by a business person.
Entrepreneur An enterprising person who is willing to take risks.
Exclusive contract An agreement that excludes others from entering the same agreement.
Executive director A director who works for a company. A non-executive director is a member of the board but is not employed by the company. See also Directors.
Financial To do with money.
Financial director An executive responsible for financial planning, making and receiving payments, and keeping records. The finance department includes accountants and bookkeepers.
Franchise A special agreement or licence granted by a company (the franchisor) to a smaller business (the franchisee) allowing it to manufacture or sell goods or a service invented or owned by the franchisor.
Free market Country or group of countries that allow businesses to operate without state control or interference, and to trade without customs duties on goods.
Goods Things other than food produced by a business.
Gross See Net and gross.
Growth Expansion of a business to increase profits.
Human resources The people

who work for a business. Also called staff or personnel.
Image How a company is seen by the public.
Incentive Payment or privilege given to make workers produce more.
Interest Money paid to investors for use of the money they have lent.
Invest To put money into a business or buy shares in it. The sum of money invested is called an investment.
Labour A collective name for workers, especially manual workers.
Labour intensive Process that demands a large number of workers.
Licence Permit that allows, for example, a franchisee to sell the franchisor's product.
Livery Distinctive uniform, colours or markings.
Logo (short for logogram) A sign or symbol that represents a word and is often used as a trademark.
Manager A person who controls or organizes a business or part of it. A person who organizes staff.
Market The total number of buyers and sellers of a product.
Marketing All the activities involved in putting a product on the market, including research and development, distribution and sales, pricing and promotion.
Market research Surveying people's tastes and requirements to assess the demand for a product.
Mass market The majority of the population. Mostly low-priced products sell to the mass market.
Merchandising The process of marketing a product or, more specifically, the use of logos or popular characters to sell products.
Net and gross A gross amount is money paid or earned before tax and other contributions have been deducted to leave a net amount.
Non-executive director See Executive director.
Overheads General costs, such as rent, heating, stationery and so on, that do not relate to a specific operation or item.
Patent An official government document that establishes an individual's or company's exclusive right or title to an invention for a certain period.
Pension scheme A method of saving money to provide a retirement income. Often both employers and employees contribute.
Pharmacist Person who makes up and sells medicines and drugs.
Physical resources Things such as buildings, machines and raw materials that a business uses.
Plant A factory, or machinery used in a factory.
Point of sale The place where a sale takes place, usually a shop.
Price The amount of money for which something can be bought or sold. Price is usually determined by supply and demand.
Private company A company that is owned by an individual or group of individuals, and whose shares are not traded on the stock exchange. See also Public company.
Product The thing that a business sells. Products can be goods or services.
Profit The difference between what a company earns – its income – and its costs.
Profit-sharing scheme The distribution of some of a company's profits to its employees, either as shares or as a bonus (an extra lump sum of money).
Promotion 1 Moving up the employment scale to a better job. 2 Promoting sales by advertising, publicity and other sales incentives such as giveaway promotional items.
Prosecution Taking legal proceedings against somebody.
Public company A business that offers shares of itself for sale to the general public.
Public relations Department of a company responsible for making sure that the company's relations with the general public are good.
Redundant A worker whose job no longer exists and has to leave the company is said to be redundant.
Retailer Business such as a shop or supermarket that sells goods in small numbers to customers. Retailers generally buy their goods from wholesalers who buy in bulk from manufacturers.
Salary Money paid in fixed amounts, usually monthly, to 'white-collar' workers.
Sales forecast Estimate of the likely number of sales to be made during a given period, based on experience and market condition.
Senior vice-president See Corporate officers.
Service Providing help rather than goods.
Shareholder A person who owns shares in a company.
Shares Tiny portions of a company's capital value. The price at which shares are bought and sold goes up and down according to the company's success. See also Stock.
Slogan A spoken or written phrase used in advertisements to help fix a product in the mind of a listener or reader.
Sponsorship Providing money or other assistance for sporting, charitable or cultural events.
State control Regulation of industry and other areas by the government.
Stock 1 Products stored ready for sale by a company. Also called inventory in the US. 2 A block of shares.
Stock market Exchange where stocks and shares are bought and sold.
Stockholder Person who holds stock.
Subsidiary A business controlled by another business. It may be partly or wholly owned.
Tax Money that businesses and individuals have to pay the government from their earnings.
Trademark A name, design, symbol or some distinguishing mark that makes a company or product unique and recognizable.
Transaction The performance of a piece of business, such as a sale.
Treasurer Another name for the financial director or chief accountant of a company. See Corporate officers; Directors.
Vice-president Person responsible to a senior vice-president or to the board of directors for work done by people under his or her supervision.
Wages Weekly payment of hourly rate paid to 'blue-collar' (manual) workers.
Wholesaler See Retailer.

Index

Numbers in *italics* indicate pictures and diagrams; those in **bold** indicate panel references.